The Importance of Living Happy

30 Ways to Do It

Sally Huss

Reviews

"Sally Huss is one of those wise people who shows you that happiness is there for you if you insist upon it. It's a matter of attitude to see the light coming into your life. Her exercises will help you create your own sunshine." -- Bill Zimmerman, Author of *A BOOK OF SUNSHINE AND LIFELINES: A BOOK OF HOPE*.

"Happiness works for me on and off the tennis court. *GET HAPPY! BE HAPPY! STAY HAPPY!* Sally tells you how in her book *THE IMPORTANCE OF LIVING HAPPY* and it will keep you smiling wherever you are. Well done, Sally!" -- Billie Jean King, Co-Founder of World Team Tennis.

"Yes, there are a million reasons to be happy and Sally Huss is number one on my list. Sally has a unique way of seeing the world and thankfully she shares her insights and wisdom with us. I like the practical way that Sally has of giving us a "learn to be happy assignment" to test our own life or to pass on to our children. Being happy is a meaningful and profound way of looking at life. Allowing ourselves to be happy is one of life's greatest gifts and Sally's mission to brighten the world one person at a time is welcome in these times more than ever. Thank you, Sally, for being the messenger." -- Kae Schreiber, Consultant to the stars

Happiness is not only one's birthright, but it is also one's duty. You see a happy person makes a happy home. A happy home promotes a happy neighborhood. Such a neighborhood affects a city, which in turn inspires a state. A happy state touches a nation. A happy nation helps create a happy world. So, being a happy person is the most important thing in the world!

Table of Contents -- 30 Ways to Live Happy

4. The Package -- Surprises keep you alert

5. The Boxing Glove -- Knowing all are great always

6. The Candle -- Remaining young eternally

7. The Racket -- Giving and Receiving freely

8. The Profile -- Looking forward to endless possibilities

9. The Mask -- Seeing the essence, or heart, of the matter

10. The Maypole -- Being free forever

11. The Bell -- Hearing the truth at all times

12. The Fist -- Using your will for good

13. The Eyes -- Seeing goodness in everything

14. The Butterfly -- Transforming all situations into good situations

15. The Light Bulb -- Following your hunches

16. The Whistle -- Bringing out the best in others

17. The Basketball Hoop -- Tending to your goals

18. The Man -- Learning to love and appreciate all people

19. The Hoe -- Knowing that your greatness is more than the work you do

20. The Door -- Opportunities come with the opening and closing of doors

21. The Air -- Learning to breathe in, any quality you need

22. The Clown -- Laughing yourself into happiness

23. The Book -- Right thinking changes everything

Preface

There are a million reasons to be happy. All of them are good! What are the circumstances that make you happy? How would you like to be happy all the time and under all circumstances? This is not only possible, it is essential, as you will learn by reading on.

The truth is, happiness is one's true nature, but it is seldom realized completely or maintained continuously. People tend to fall in and out of happiness as they fall in and out of love. The secret is to know where happiness comes from and how to maintain it by removing all obstacles that get in its way.

Most people wait for something to happen to make them happy. The truth is that if you wait to be happy, you will wait forever. If, however, you are happy now, you will be happy forever. The key is to know how to be happy now. That is what this book is for. Use as directed and live happily ever after!

How to Use this Book

This book is designed to lead you to a greater sense of happiness. It contains thirty extraordinary and fun exercises that you can do to raise your level of happiness, regardless of circumstances. These exercises help you develop sure-fire skills to removing any obstacle that gets in the way of your natural state. Go through the exercises, one day at a time.

Each exercise has a special symbol attached to it. It represents your work, your play, your theme, your practice, your exercise for that day to improve your state of happiness. Note the number of times you need to repeat the exercise during the day. These are heart-expanding exercises. They are very powerful and will lead to your becoming a powerhouse of happiness. Each time you have completed the exercise, you are to say the affirmation assigned to that symbol, either aloud or silently (aloud is better.) Then add the following words: "I am a happy person. The happier I am, the happier I get," and feel it!

"Feel it?" you ask. "How do I feel happy when nothing has occurred to make me feel happy?"

Ah, that is the trick! In order to feel happy, you need to know what happiness is and where it comes from. Make this statement: "I am (state your name)" and point to yourself. **Do this now**! Do not read on until you have made this statement and pointed to yourself.

Notice that in identifying yourself you have pointed to the center of your chest area. It is a universal phenomenon that when a person points to him or herself, he or she points to this spot. It is the heart center, not the physical heart that pumps blood, but the emotional or spiritual heart center that pumps life – or love. Where there is love there is happiness. Where there is happiness there is love. The heart center is where happiness comes from. This is where happiness resides.

To prove the point, if you touch this spot and smile, good feeling will pour forth. In fact, it is almost impossible not to feel good when concentrating on the heart center. Even a thought of the heart center, plus a smile, will evoke good feeling.

It is important to note, however, that the heart center has a door on it. In ordinary people, the door opens and closes depending on circumstances or happenings, but it remains open all the time in extraordinary people. Anybody can become extraordinary by learning how to keep this heart center open. This is how you "feel it," and feeling it is essential to learning how to live happily, even in difficult times.

So when you have completed one of your daily exercises, concentrate on the heart center and smile. Now that you have the heart center open, you wish to make a mental picture of yourself taking a large pot of flowers and propping it open permanently. After all, once you've got it open, no sense in closing it!

Fulfill your daily assignment by completing the number of times you are to practice the exercise. Go through all thirty exercises, one per day. When you have completed them all, you may wish to repeat any that need honing or any that seem to help you overcome any difficulty that gets in the way of your feeling good.

Now it is time to begin. To briefly review:

1. Follow the directions for the exercise, making sure to note the number of times you are to repeat the exercise that day.

2. Say the suggested symbol statement aloud when you've finished one of the exercises, adding: "I am a happy person. The happier I am, the happier I get!"

3. Feel it. Feel happy by concentrating on the heart center and smiling.

4. Repeat the exercise as many times as indicated.

5. Continue for thirty days.

6. Live happily ever after!

1. The Sun

The sun is your symbol today. The sun is your guide, your teacher, and your model. The sun is a brilliant being. As we all know, yet sometimes do not acknowledge, we live by its generosity and warmth.

Study the sun, and you will find that the sun shines equally on everyone. It plays no favorites. It does not care about what you do, the color of your skin, the level of your education or finances, your home or shelter, your car or clothing. It shines the same on each and every one of us. Even when there are clouds in the sky and people cannot see the sun, it remains high above the clouds, still shining.

You should be grateful to the sun. Through its shining it gives life to everything on earth. All people, plants, and animals owe their existence to the sun. It, however, does not seem to matter to the sun whether we are aware of this. It just keeps shining. That is its purpose. It is in the business of shining.

Each person has a drop of sunlight in his or her heart and has the same ability as the sun – to shine and spread light. By exercising this inborn ability, the sun within can become as powerful as the sun without.

This is your assignment today: shine equally on everyone, including the person you see in the mirror. Find six instances during the day in which you consciously give your attention, your sunshine, to someone you would normally overlook. Take a moment with a cashier at a supermarket check stand, feel kindly toward an unseen voice on the phone, or have a conversation with the shyest child in a group. There are endless situations where you have the opportunity to study your own preferences and rise above the ordinary, human state to a much higher, sunnier state.

Say the following symbol statement each time you complete one of the six assigned exercises, *"I shine like the sun. I shine equally on everyone! I am a happy person. The happier I am, the happier I get!"* Smile and shine!

2. The Bee

Today your symbol is the bee. The bee represents the Law of Attraction. You attract in your life what you "vibrate to" in the form of people and circumstances. The bee is attracted to all that is fragrant and sweet. Study the Law of Attraction today in all of its forms. Everything that happens to you or to anyone else is the result of this ongoing, never-changing law. Find seven instances of the workings of this law today.

Examples of this law in action might be found in your residence, your job, the people in your life, even the clothing and colors worn by you and others. Are they bright or are they dull? Is there harmony and peacefulness around the people you study? Do they radiate hope or do they dampen your spirits?

If you wish to improve your circumstances in the future, you must first elevate your vibration. Your vibration is your "hum" or your "purr" level on the happiness scale, which runs from very unhappy to very happy to bliss. Whatever you seek or want – whether it is a new car, a good job, a lovely home, a true love, or even the opportunity to help others – the motive behind it is always to improve your own state of happiness. Be happy first, and all good things will come to you.

Today's symbol statement is, *"Today I control my destiny by sending out what I want to come back to me – happiness! I am a happy person. The happier I am, the happier I get!"* Smile and feel it!

3. The Bicycle

In life, pedaling is that constant, even quality of riding easily with the highs and lows of the world outside. Today you get to ride the bicycle. The bicycle represents equanimity – the quality of being even-tempered. On a bicycle you have to keep pedaling to stay upright. The terrain is usually uphill or downhill from where you are, but the pedaling must always continue, no matter your speed or surroundings.

Pedaling is the action of your inner, calm center, which remains unperturbed by the frazzle and dazzle of daily happenings. It is like a heartbeat. It can be counted on, and relied upon, to be steady. It is a very desirable quality.

As you go through today, develop this characteristic if you don't have it, and use it if you do. Keep pedaling; the scenery is forever changing. The scenery might be disappointments at work, triumphs at home, a loss on the golf course, or the promise of an exotic vacation.

Find six instances during the day in which you keep pedaling as the circumstances around you rise and fall. Pedal at your own pace. Let your center remain undisturbed.

The symbol statement for this exercise is, *"I remain balanced as I pedal through the highs and lows of life. I am a happy person. The happier I am, the happier I get!"* Smile and feel it!

4. The Package

Today you are given the package. The package is a mystery package. It represents the unplanned, the unexpected – a surprise!

Life is full of surprises. They happen all the time in our daily lives. They keep our routine not so routine. No matter how much we plan and design our day, surprises continue to pop up.

It is obvious that we cannot control everything that happens to us, only our attitude toward these events.

And, the best attitude to have toward a surprise is that it is a gift, a present. It is the opportunity to learn something, the opportunity to be generous, to meet someone new, to perform a good deed.

When the car won't start, when Johnny has spilled his apple juice, when you've lost a tennis match to a lesser player, you have been given an opportunity in disguise to expand yourself. This expansion may be in the form of the opportunity to practice patience, to delight in another's success or develop flexibility. Take the surprise package, the unexpected situation, and see it as a gift – find something useful in the challenge presented to you.

Find three instances today in which something out of the ordinary happens, and then see each as a gift. Respond with the right attitude – greet surprises with open arms.

Your symbol statement for today is, *"I love surprises. They keep me on my toes! I am a happy person. The happier I am, the happier I get!* Smile and feel it!

5. The Boxing Glove

Your symbol today is the boxing glove. The boxing glove represents self-worth. The great boxing champion Muhammad Ali used to say, "I am the greatest!" He was and so are you.

You are greater than anything you can imagine. Your greatness is beyond your own comprehension. You may be blind to your own limitlessness and value.

Today, live with this idea: "I am the greatest! There is none greater!" See how it affects your life.

The boxing glove also symbolizes fighting. Often people are at war with themselves. They take little jabs at themselves, put themselves down. This self-critical treatment affects their spirit, lowers their self-esteem and their state of happiness. These actions are neither useful, nor helpful, nor true, and are definitely forbidden.

One person may mess up or make more mistakes. Another may be brighter, prettier, faster; he or she may jump higher, play better bridge, write better, cook better, sell better, have more money or more friends. But no one is greater than another! Each of us is great, and all of us are greater than anything we can imagine.

Observe how you and others value yourselves through words and actions. Find four distinct statements or actions made by you or someone else that reveal self-worth. Do they know they are great? Do you know you are great?

Improve the value you give yourself. Raise your self-esteem by using the following symbol statement, *"I am the greatest. There is none greater. I am a happy person. The happier I am, the happier I get!* Smile and feel it!

6. The Candle

The candle is a birthday candle. How old are you today? Whatever age you are, today you are as young as you will ever be. That makes you young eternally!

Pick your perfect age and stay there forever. Your mind and feelings can be any age you choose. Do not be put off by birth certificates or images in a mirror. Outsides change. What is inside stays the same. Make what is inside your perfect age and you will not only be young at heart, you will be young and smart.

Today, find a couple of situations in which you catch yourself thinking or acting in a manner different than you would like, just because you think you are "too old" to do otherwise. Then, change it. It may be in the clothes you choose to wear, the food you eat, the gait of your walk, or the manner you deal with others. Is the food boring? Are your clothes fun to wear? Are you light-hearted or heavy-handed? The symbol statement is, *"Today I'm as young as I'll ever be. That makes me young eternally. I am a happy person The happier I am, the happier I get!"* Smile and feel it!

7. The Racket

The racket represents the game of tennis. Tennis is one of the greatest sports in the world. To play tennis well requires the total involvement of all aspects of a person – physical, mental, and emotional. You must have endurance and agility, be intellectually bright and crafty, and have grace and a great heart.

One of the most delightful qualities of tennis is that it is based on giving and receiving – or serving and receiving. As you probably know, during a tennis match, one player serves to the other and receives the service from the other. Serving and receiving occur equally. The players take turns. The game is fair. It is balanced.

In life, too, giving and receiving must be balanced. People are happiest when this takes place. There are, no doubt, people in your circle whom you may consider to be great givers – very generous, as well as people you know who are considered to be "takers." It is important to be both a good giver and a good receiver. Many times the givers feel unworthy of receiving, so they only wish to give. In doing so, they do not allow another to give. It is as important to receive well as it is to give generously. It allows the other person to earn his or her brownie points. The takers, or those who only receive, deny themselves the pleasure you can derive from giving.

Naturally, at certain times in your life, you may become very needy and be forced to accept the generosity offered by someone else, such as during an illness or hard times. Soon, however, the sneaker will be on the other foot and an opportunity will arise where you can give again and balance the equation.

Study the concept of give and take, of serving and receiving, in different aspects of your life. It might be in your daily activities or in something as simple as a conversation. Be conscious of it six times today – three for giving and three for receiving. Feel the enjoyment of being a player on either side of the net.

Say the following symbol statement, *"I am a great player in the game of life. I give and receive freely. I am a happy person. The happier I am, the happier I get!"* Smile and feel it!

8. The Profile

By studying the profile we observe that the eyes are on the front of the head. The eyes are on the front of the head so that we can see where we are going and not be bothered by what is past. The profile represents one's natural state of looking ahead.

What is past is past and can never return unless we turn our eyes inward to look at an old memory. As soon as we do this, we cannot see what is actually before us at any given moment. The truth is that we can deal with only what is before us. We cannot deal with what has already been done.

Many times it is with guilt or regret of some kind that we look back, rehashing old situations and trying to make events come out differently. Guilt causes us to blame ourselves or someone else for what went wrong. Guilt, however, is the guilty party. Give it the boot! Get it out of your life forever! It is the thief of *now* and *now* is all we have. Now is a gift of surprises waiting to be explored this very moment.

Today, find five instances in which you are aware that your attention has moved backward in time to the rehash pile. Smile, and quickly bring your attention forward, knowing that you have learned something from your past experience.

Life is a big school. You go to school to learn, but you will miss the lesson of today if you are thumbing through yesterday's quizzes.

Your exercise may be used in many areas of your life. Rehashing can occur in disagreements with a good friend, on a golf course over the last shot, or in a business call over a sales presentation.

Remain in your natural state – eyes forward, chin up! Your symbol statement today is, *"I look forward to the possibilities before me! I am a happy person The happier I am, the happier I get!"* Smiles and feel it!

9. The Mask

The mask represents the outer surface, the outward shell of a person. It consists not only of your physical makeup, but your personality's makeup too.

Everyone has a mask of sorts, which covers the true self – the heart. One of the keys to happiness is having good relationships with others, and the secret to this is to focus on the heart. Forget a person's skin. Forget the face. Forget the form. Forget the size and age. Forget the way, and way beyond the skin, love the within. Love the heart.

Just as the surfaces of different materials can scratch, the surfaces of people – their personalities – can be abrasive as well. But when you communicate from your heart to the heart of another, you will always find common ground that is soft and comfortable.

All relationships – family, friends, and business – are better when the masks are overlooked and the heart is seen. Your relationship with yourself is also greatly improved by giving less attention to the outer shell and listening to your own heart instead.

Today, forget the mask, forget the skin, and love the within – the heart – with as many people as you can. Find at least six examples in which you see through the mask and deal directly heart to heart. You will find the whole experience heart-warming.

Today, the symbol statement is, *"Nothing fools me. I always deal with the heart of the matter. I am a happy person. The happier I am, the happier I get!"* Smile and feel it!

10. The Maypole

The symbol today is the maypole. A maypole is a tall pole decorated with streamers on top, which May Day celebrants hold while dancing. These dancers, dressed in brightly colored costumes with flowers in their hair, hold the streamers in their hands, and through patterned maneuvers and dance steps, weave their way around the maypole, braiding the streamers around the pole as they go. It is a very beautiful ceremony.

The maypole, with its streamers, represents all of the possible personality traits a person can have, along with their ensuing potential entanglements. Personality traits can be positive, like bravery, generosity, grace, kindness, politeness, and eagerness. And they can be negative, as seen in jealousy, cowardliness, greediness, rudeness, crudeness, laziness, self-righteousness, and so forth.

It is helpful to know that all personality traits are universal. They belong to everyone. More precisely, their availability belongs to everyone to use if they choose. The maypole and its streamers of traits are ever-floating in the air for anyone to grab onto or let go of as we choose.

It is a common mistake to assume that we are the creators of these traits, especially if they are of a negative nature. Take jealousy, for example. You feel jealous over the attentions or fortunes of another and consequently become entangled in the web of trying to cover up these envious feelings. How to get out of the entanglement? Let go! Choose another trait!

Just as you may take responsibility for the creation of jealousy, you may also take pride in ownership of an admired trait such as generosity or politeness. Better to give up the idea of self-creation and simply enjoy the traits that you have chosen. Pick the sweetest apples in the basket, the prettiest streamers as they float by, and live weight-free and carefree.

As you go through your day today, find six situations in which you observe personality traits in action, in either yourself or someone else. Let go of the traits you don't want and hang onto the traits you do want. See all personality traits as floating, independent of yourself, but always available for use.

By seeing others as independent of these traits as well, you allow them the freedom to change easily, too. The symbol statement for this exercise is, *"I am free to be what I want to be and act the way I want to act. I am a happy person. The happier I am, the happier I get!"* Smile and feel it!

11. The Bell

The bell is the Liberty Bell and represents truth and freedom. Truth, liberty and happiness go hand in hand. Without truth there is no liberty. You forever cover up what you are not truthful about in your life, which creates a heavy burden to carry around. The truth, however, sets you free. There is no weight to being truthful, no planning ahead: no maneuvering, scheming, or avoiding.

When you deal with life truthfully, you are at ease, free, and we all need this atmosphere of freedom – of liberty – to be happy. So, truth is what we seek.

Like a bell, a person needs to be tuned – tuned to truth. This is accomplished by speaking the truth, hearing it, and living it. Truth has a resonance all its own. It is loud and clear. You can't miss it, and by acting truthfully, other people will respond in turn to you with their own honesty. Truth is good for everybody. Fess up at all times.

Today, be conscious of expressing your true thoughts and feelings when asked, and then act on these truths. Find seven instances during the day in which you honor the truth through your speech and actions. It might be a simple statement, such as "I like this pear!" Being truthful is a good habit to have, and it can be addictive. When you are truthful about the little things in life, you will know the truth about the bigger things when you hear them.

Today's symbol statement is, *"The sound of truth is music to my ears. I am a happy person. The happier I am, the happier I get!"* Smile and feel it!

12. The Fist

Today your symbol is the fist. The fist represents willpower – the power to do or not to do, the power to go or to stay, the power of choice.

You have your own will, and because it is your will, you can do with it what you please. Your will is your way, your choice. In most situations, there is a choice of what to do – to do something useful or not useful, good or bad, or to do nothing at all. Doing something good is naturally the thing to do, but sometimes you may find yourself in a situation in which you don't know what is right or are afraid of doing what is wrong, and so you do nothing at all. It is far better to make a wrong decision and be in action than not to participate at all. Wrong decisions reveal themselves in time, and corrections can be made. When no action is taken, nothing is learned. Nothing ventured, nothing gained!

Whereas the will in willpower is choice, the power in willpower is force. This force is everywhere. It belongs to everyone. It is ever-present, ever-lasting, ever-plentiful. All you have to do is use it. Just take the amount you need.

Many people have the misconception that certain individuals have stronger wills than others. Not so. They have simply used their will to harness the available force in a greater amount than have others, and made a habit of it. It is there for the taking.

Some people choose not to exercise their will. They go along with the crowd, even when they know it is not best. They tend to be passive will-o'-the-wisps, waiting for the next breeze to blow them in some direction. A person, who knows his or her own heart, picks a direction, uses his or her will for good, and then powers up – he or she can go anywhere and do anything!

Today, explore your will and make sure what you are doing is what you want to do. Be willful and align your will consciously with that which you know is good. Find three instances today to test your willpower. If you play tennis today, will yourself to play tennis with great force and enthusiasm. The will lines up all of your energies and gets your horsepower revved up and moving in one direction. You will be a dynamo on the court or off.

Say the following symbol statement, *"I will to do what is good and I have endless power to do it! I am a happy person. The happier I am, the happier I get!"* Smile and feel it!

13. The Eyes

The eyes see. To improve one's state of happiness, the eyes need to see that which is good.

The eyes see, but it is how they interpret what they see that affects our true vision. The interpretation must come from a positive point of view. How can we do this when much of life seems so helter-skelter, so disruptive and destructive?

You must trust that life is really very orderly and that a much higher power than our own has everything under control. Even if you do not know the master plan of this higher power, it is comforting to live with the idea that there is such a plan and that each of us is included in it.

From a human point of view, you cannot see all the pieces of the puzzle and how they fit together comfortably. The only option is to raise your sights to higher ground and look at the world from that vantage point.

By incorporating this view into your own life, you will find its truth proven time and again. Find five situations during the day in which you encounter something you would normally consider "bad" and change your view of it -- knowing that there must be a very good reason for it. It might be a "disaster" on TV, a missed appointment, a "bad" weather forecast, or anything to which your immediate reaction is "I wish it were otherwise."

By viewing life and all of its activities as good, your life and all of your activities will improve.

Use the following symbol statement, *"I see only good and it is good enough for me! I am a happy person. The happier I am, the happier I get!"* Smile and feel it!

14. The Butterfly

The butterfly is your symbol today. The butterfly represents transformation. The butterfly is a being that has been transformed from a rather unattractive caterpillar into a very beautiful winged flower.

We are constantly transforming things, whether we are aware of it or not. We take lettuce, celery, cucumber, radish, tomato, and green pepper, and make a salad. If we eat the salad, we transform plant matter into the animal matter of our bodies. In the same way, we take trees and transform them into lumber, which, in turn, is transformed into houses. We take houses or apartments, and with some effort and furnishings, transform them into homes. An artist takes an empty canvas and turns it into a painting that can be hung in the home.

Dentists, hairdressers, dog groomers, secretaries, counselors, plumbers, real estate agents, coaches, and almost any other professional you can imagine are in the business of transforming people or things. Our work as human beings is to transform things for the better. Not everyone has this straight yet. We are here to help out in any way, at any moment -- even if it is just to pick up a dirty sock and throw it in a hamper.

Your exercise for the day is to be aware of the transformation that continually goes on around you and to make four concerted efforts at positive transformation in your life. It may be to straighten a room, organize a garage, or clean a purse. It may be to make a special dish for dinner. It may also take the form of transforming a situation, such as smoothing out a conflict between colleagues, elevating the mood of a friend, or changing the atmosphere in a room by changing the channel on the TV to a more uplifting program. You will find countless ways to transform situations for the better in your daily life.

The symbol statement for this exercise is, *"I am a walking, talking, creative transformer for good! I am a happy person. The happier I am, the happier I get!* Smile and feel it!

15. The Light Bulb

The light bulb represents intuition, as in bright ideas. Intuition is that sixth sense of knowing without knowing why you know. It is a knowing beyond the rational mind, and it is a far higher faculty than logical reasoning. Intuition should be listened to and followed unquestionably because its truth comes from a universal level of awareness, whereas reason comes from a more limited, personal level of knowledge.

Following intuition's lead takes you down the path of least resistance. There, you find the door of opportunity opened to you often, just where you wouldn't expect it to be. Intuition consists of those thoughts and feelings that pop up unexpectedly and seem too good to be true, but if followed, prove to be divinely designed. Never pass up a good hunch. Never question why your eyes seem to rest on a license plate or a billboard or a page in a book with just the right message for you. A higher power of communication is operating. Listen up. Let yourself be inspired!

By following your own feelings of intuition, your life will be spontaneous and fun; it will take on a magical quality. Use your intuition in any area of your life today. You may decide to go out to dinner tonight. Does a new restaurant come to mind? Do you have the inclination to call an old friend for no particular reason? Do it. Would you like to take a nap, but have too much to do? Sleep on it!

Find four instances today in which you "sense," rather than "reason," what is best in a situation. Intuition is really that which is in your heart. That is where the great communicator of inspired thoughts resides.

Your symbol statement for this exercise is, *"I never miss a trick because I never pass up a hunch! I am a happy person. The happier I am, the happier I get!* Smile and feel it!

16. The Whistle

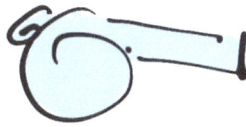

The whistle belongs to the coach. A coach believes in the greatness of his or her players, and then coaxes it out of them. So, the whistle represents this quality of looking for the best in others and helping to bring it forth. Nothing really makes you happier than to help another. Coaching greatness is the perfect opportunity.

Greatness is inbred. It is in all of us. Greatness can be detected in many different forms and abilities. But many of us don't believe in our greatness and need some coaching to bring it out.

How can you help? Volunteer. When you do, you find that your greatness as a coach surfaces. Encourage a friend to find a better job, one that fits his or her talents. Ask a child to work on dinner plans and prepare the meal with you. Inspire a teenager to extend him or herself on a school project rather than just do enough to get by. Compliment an older neighbor on his or her garden. Acknowledge and support greatness wherever you can.

If we all take it upon ourselves to help bring out the best in others, there will be such greatness exposed and explored that we will be amazed at the harmony we can create in our own lives – and in the world. Mothers and fathers are natural coaches. Teachers are professional coaches. Join the coaching staff. Be a coach today.

Find five opportunities today to practice your coaching skills on someone with hidden greatness.

The symbol statement for today is, *"I am a great coach. I bring out the best in others. I am a happy person. The happier I am, the happier I get!"* Smile and feel it!

17. The Basketball Hoop

The basketball hoop represents goaltending or guarding the goal. In basketball, goaltending is illegal; but in real life goaltending is not only legal, it is a very wise move. If you don't attend to your own goals, no one else will and nothing will get accomplished.

Setting goals is important. It sets a direction for your life. It charts your course and focuses your actions. People are always in action. The secret is to have those actions accomplish something you desire. Your desires may be related to your health, business, family relationships, and so on.

A smile with feeling connects the heart to action, thus empowering you and adds the power to make things come true.

Today, if you do not have any goals, set some. If you do, attend to them by taking action to bring them to fulfillment. Take three actions to accomplish your goal or goals today. For example, set up appointments for a new job you are seeking, work the garden and mow the lawn to get the house ready for sale, or write a chapter in a book you wish to complete.

Say the following symbol statement, *"I tend to my goal; they gets me where I want to go. I am a happy person. The happier I am, the happier I get!* Smile and feel it!

18. The Man

Your symbol today is the man. The man represents humanity. Every person on earth is part of this whole that we call humanity – no one is left out. Each of us is like one little cell of a great big being. Each cell, or person, has a meaningful part to play, a significant job to do, which only he or she can do to maintain and improve the state of humanity.

On this day, feel a part of this whole, feel connected to others whose paths you cross. Do this by making the assumption that we are all part of one being. We belong to each other, regardless of our differences. And, we are all working together in various areas of our lives on the same project – the improvement of humanity and its relationship to the world.

Today, find four opportunities to express this unity with words or actions. Act and speak as if you are in the presence of family, even if you are in the presence of strangers. As you know, the tie that binds families is love, and everyone is at ease with family. Silently love a stranger and you will have expanded your family, or more accurately, made yourself aware of the family of man that already exists.

Make this your symbol statement for today, *"I love people. The more people I love, the more people love me. I am a happy person. The happier I am, the happier I get!* Smile and feel it!

19. The Hoe

Today your symbol is the hoe. The hoe represents work. Everyone needs to work – needs to have something of value to do. The hoe denotes physical work, but there is mental work, too. Doctors, lawyers, accountants, teachers, writers, salespeople, securities brokers, counselors, and many others work with their minds more than their bodies. Gardeners, letter carriers, baseball players, housekeepers, mechanics, plumbers, and so forth work more with their bodies. Some work pays well in terms of money. Some work pays nothing in terms of money, like the work that mothers or students do. We all need to have work. It is our *raison d'etre*, and it gives us a sense of purpose.

Like everything else, working requires the right attitude. Many folks become so involved in their work, so desperate for success, so hungry for profit, or so desirous of approval from a superior, that they only identify themselves with the outcome of their work. It is important to give your all, but at the same time keep a check on your ambitions.

Be aware today, as you do your job, that judgment of your work is not a judgment of yourself. Find four examples of your daily duties in which you can evaluate what you do and then make sure you separate it from who you are. Perhaps the lasagna didn't come out as well as you would have liked or you left out some details in a marketing plan. Some days you do not find the computer friendly. Other days every aspect of your work is friendly. Even when your proposal is a huge success, remember that it may be great, but you are greater.

Today, say the following symbol statement, *"My work is something I do, not what I am. What I am is far greater than anything I can do."* And be sure to add, *"I am a happy person. The happier I am, the happier I get!"* Smile and feel it!

20. The Door

The door represents opportunity. Doors open and close. Life is constantly revealing the best path to take, the safest route, the surest road to success – the straight line to happiness. It is our job to follow it.

We often have many plans in different areas of our lives, all in motion simultaneously. At the right time and in the right way, a door will open to complete a plan, fulfill a dream, or answer a prayer. To move on, to move ahead, doors need to close. But as surely as one door closes, another will open.

It is important not to try to enter a door that is closed to you. Forced entry is unlawful on any level and can lead to being in the wrong place at the wrong time. But, to waltz through an open door that is just waiting for you, makes you feel very welcomed indeed. You know you've come to the right place. You know you've done the right thing, and good results will surely follow.

Today, find one instance where a door has been closed to you and another where a door has been opened for you. They do not have to be linked. More than likely they won't be, as it may take some time for a new opportunity to reveal itself after a door has been shut.

Closed doors are experienced in losing a job or not getting a job, not making a sale, not finding the dress you want in the size you want, not making the basketball team, or not selling your house in a tough market. Opened doors happen when someone suggests a new job or business to start, your child joins the school choir, a new recipe is received, or you are given approval to refinance or lease your home.

Doors of opportunity can be big or small – they all have to do with improving your circumstances. They might even be as tiny as finding a quarter on the sidewalk.

Today's symbol statement is, *"When one door closes, another door opens. I am a happy person. The happier I am, the happier I get! Smile and feel it!*

21. The Air

Today your symbol is the air. Notice that this symbol is filled with dots. These dots represent everything that is in the air. Air looks empty, but it is not. It is full of the subtlest essences of life. Air is nourishment for the highest part of ourselves, as well as the denser, physical part. Man cannot live without air.

Beyond the physical attributes of air, all that a person could ever want or need in the realm of higher qualities exists in the air, too. Courage, strength, love, forgiveness, peace, empathy, sympathy, and grace are in the air. All a person has to do is breathe it in.

Discover this warehouse of riches as you go about your breathing today. Call upon these higher qualities to clear the air in any area of your life. Breathe in whatever you need at the moment, as you would breathe in perfume. Do you need patience with your children? Sympathy for an ill friend? Do you lack courage to tackle a special assignment at work? All these special qualities are there in the air in endless supply. Use this technique eight times today. You may wish to use it more.

Use this symbol statement, *"A wealth of richness surrounds me. I inhale what I need in the air I breathe. I am a happy person. The happier I am, the happier I get!"* Smile and feel it!

22. The Clown

The clown represents laughter. Today, laugh as much as you can. Exercise your funny bone. Sometimes it gets out of shape and needs a good workout. Today is the day. Do it. Laugh! Laugh at everything on your path worth laughing at or with. Any excuse will do. Once you focus on laughter, you will not believe how many amusing situations arise. Give in. Laugh. Life's little absurdities and oddities are your opportunity to rise to the occasion by bubbling up with laughter.

In Japan, and probably in China too, there is a special sect of monks who begin each day's meditation with a half hour of laughter. For the monks, studying light in all its forms includes light-heartedness.

Many doctors have found that laughter is indeed the best medicine and have even prescribed comedy films for their patients to watch. It seems that after much scientific study researchers have determined that laughter releases some highly beneficial chemicals in the body that assist in healing. Of course, everyone feels better when they laugh. Laughter makes you happy, and when you are happy everything is right with the world.

The symbol statement for this exercise is, "*I love to laugh. The more I laugh the happier I am. I am a happy person. The happier I am, the happier I get!*" Feel it and laugh!

23. The Book

You have opened this book today. To understand a book, you must think. So, the book is the symbol that represents thinking. It is important to understand how thinking works. Simply stated, it works like this: As you think, so it will be! (At least, so it will be to you.) Life constantly manifests your thinking for you. Life brings your thoughts right out in front and puts them in your face. You cannot escape your thinking. It is mirrored in the happenings and relationships in your life.

Fortunately, life is based on good, whether you think so or not, and life reveals this truth overwhelmingly if you believe it to be true. However, if you choose to think otherwise, life will certainly oblige you in this thinking. For instance, if you think it is difficult to find a job, it will be. If you think dogs don't like you, they certainly won't. If you think you can't find a man or woman to love, you will have your proof. Change such thoughts and you will change your life.

Not only will your life rise to your thought level, your children and others around you will rise to your thought level. If you hold to the idea that they are capable and responsible, they will prove it. Everything starts with a thought, so make it a good one.

Find six examples today that show how thinking manifests itself and that "right" thinking matters. Pay attention to how you think about friends, family, business, school, or even about yourself. If a person thinks, "I am a procrastinator," he or she will be. If, however, a person who has been a procrastinator changes their thought to, "I am a great decision maker: I make make good choices and act on them quickly," that person will become a whirlwind at getting things done. It is the easiest way to change your life. Simply think your life better.

The symbol statement for today is, *"My life is great because I think it is. I am a happy person. The happier I am, the happier I get!* Smile and feel it!

24. The Windshield Wipers

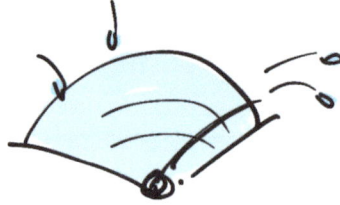

Whether it is rainy or not, the windshield wipers are your symbol for the day. Windshield wipers are used in bad weather to wipe away the rain so that you can see clearly and maneuver safely as you drive down the highway.

In the realm of the mind, there can also be bad weather consisting of negative thoughts and images. These bad weather thoughts can be old, sad, or melancholy memories; hurtful words by someone you love; mistakes you may have made; fears dancing around trying to get your goat; or temptations of all kinds that you wish would just go away. They may rain down on you from the inside, blocking your view of what is really happening. But, just like the windshield wipers on your car, blinking your eyes a couple of times quickly can clear unwanted images and thoughts from your consciousness and put you back on track.

Blinking your eyes is a very useful technique, not only for clearing old, recurring thoughts, but for adjusting your focus when you find your mind drifting from the subject at hand. This technique can also be used when there is no subject at hand and your mind need not be engaged, yet it continues to babble on anyway. In the blink of an eye (or two), the mind's screen can be cleared and inner peace restored.

Your assignment today is to use this blinking technique at least nine times. You will probably use it more. It is fun, fast, and effective.

Your symbol statement is, *"I see clearly. No thought spoils my happy point of view. I am a happy person. The happier I am, the happier I get!"* Smile and feel it!

25. The Trophy

Today you are a winner! You are awarded the trophy. Traditionally, a trophy is given to the winner of a competitive event. In this event, your life, there may or may not be other competitors. In any case, you are the main participant and the only entrant you can do anything about. So, you might as well perform like a winner.

It is your life, your game, and it is important that you play to win, give your all, do your best, and participate fully. This is what a winner does. In life, you do not have to win something to be a winner. You need only to combine a winning attitude with go-for-it action.

Practice this combination of attitude and action in any area of your life, from cleaning your house to dressing for the day to writing a letter to cooking dinner to dealing with your children. Today, practice championship abilities by finding three activities in which you consciously give your all instead of participating halfheartedly. After all, a trophy is also called "a loving cup." Give your love, which is your attention, wholeheartedly to these activities and see how much more enjoyable they become and how much better the results are. You may be surprised by how much of a winner you really are.

The symbol statement for this exercise is, *"I am a winner! My loving cup runneth over. I am a happy person. The happier I am, the happier I get!"* Smile and feel it!

26. The Flower

Today your symbol is the flower. The flower represents beauty. You can find something beautiful anywhere you look, if you are looking for something beautiful. It may reveal itself in a kind gesture of a friend, the sound of birds outside your window, fabric in a store, orderliness in an office, or a smile on a child's face.

Beauty is that heavenly quality that shines above the ordinary. It is one of the highest of all spiritual qualities because it is the manifestation of harmony. The essence of what we consider beautiful is the perfectly balanced union of all parts of a whole. A beautiful play, a beautiful rose, a beautiful symphony, a beautiful work of art, and a beautiful human being all have this quality of harmony.

Find beauty in your surroundings today. Look for beauty and find it in at least eight different forms. Consciously recognize beauty when you do find it. Sigh if you like.

Today's symbol statement is, *"Beauty surrounds me. I see it wherever I look. I am a happy person. The happier I am, the happier I get!"* Smile and feel it!

27. The Bird

The bird is the Hawaiian *iiwi* bird, and represents the action of striving.

Birds were first brought to the Hawaiian Islands by great gusts of wind across the sea. These first birds discovered the beautiful and fragrant trumpet-like flowers that flourished on the islands. These flowers, with their long, tubular petals had their nectar hidden deep at the bottom of these tubes. The birds, striving to reach this nectar, evolved so that their beaks perfectly fit the flower's curved and elongated shape.

When you have a desire for something and you strive for it, you send out energy and effort in that direction until the goal is reached. Striving is the work needed to accomplish something. Anything worth having is worth striving for, worth working for. Striving develops and hones the striver. Those who receive something without striving for it are robbed of the knowledge of their own greatness.

As you strive for and accomplish your goals, other desires will surface and other goals will form. Striving, therefore, is an ongoing process of reaching and stretching, always with the hope of making things better. A golfer for example, may first master the use of a nine iron, then a seven iron, perhaps a three iron, a two wood, and then the driver. With each club, thousands of balls must be hit, hundreds of adjustments made, but all the while, the golfer is striving to improve his overall game.

Find four instances today in which you strive toward small or large goals. They may be the efforts you make to get yourself in better shape. They may be efforts to improve your work situation by organizing your activities more efficiently. They may be efforts made to improve your home environment, such as rearranging the furniture. These are all examples of strivings for what you consider to be better.

Say the symbol statement, *"I stretch my greatness as I strive for what I want. I am a happy person. The happier I am, the happier I get!"* Smile and feel it!

28. The Star

The star is your symbol today. We love stars. They sparkle brightly and give off rays of light. We are attracted to them. We are star-gazers and star-amazers, as we watch them fill the heavens at night.

We are star-spangled. We have stars on our flag. We have stars on our soccer, baseball, basketball and football teams. We have stars on the Hollywood Walk of Fame. We have movie stars, comic stars, rock stars, and literary stars. There are TV stars and generals with four stars. We even have cookie-cutter stars that we use to fill cookie jars with cookie stars.

We put stars on our Christmas trees. There are stars of David and stars of Bethlehem and stars of India. And if we are lucky, we have stars in our eyes.

We look up to stars, but who looks up to us? The truth is that we must look up to ourselves. Each one of us must put ourselves on a pedestal. Each of us is the star of our own sitcom TV show. Play your part to the hilt! Enjoy yourself, and make it the most exciting series on the air. Win an Emmy!

Today, bask in your own glory. Treat yourself like a star. Pull out the linen napkins. Use the crystal for yourself. Get rid of old and tired-looking clothes. Let yourself sparkle. Treat yourself royally. Make the most of your business, social or family activities. Give them importance because you are important. Find four examples in which you add star power to your activities and see if your performance does not improve.

Use the symbol statement, *"I am the star of my life. I love my part and play it well! I am a happy person. The happier I am, the happier I get!"* Smile and feel it!

29. The Sailboat

The sailboat represents that place everyone is trying to reach where you can relax and enjoy life. It signifies that time when you have enough money to buy a sailboat and take a leisurely sail on a Sunday afternoon.

When is that time? When will my ship be coming in, you wonder? The time is now. It is always now, no matter what time it is. So, now is the time to relax and enjoy life. It is full of wonder in all of its forms, not just on a Sunday afternoon sail. Whatever activities you are engaged in, whether you're doing laundry, driving in traffic on the freeway, picking up the kids after school, making dinner, reading a marketing plan, devising a game plan – they are part of life and therefore worthy of great enjoyment. Jump in! Enjoy yourself! Enjoy life!

Find seven instances today in which you consciously acknowledge and enjoy your life, whether it's in the middle of discussing your proposal at work to reading a bedtime story to your child.

The symbol statement is, *"Life is wonderful! I never forget it! I am a happy person. The happier I am, the happier I get!* Smile and feel it!

30. The Heart

The heart, of course, represents love. Your love is your life, your life force, your life energy; and your life is your love. When you give your focus or your attention to something, at that moment you are giving your life to it, and, whether you know it or not, you are giving your love.

The exercise for today is to give your attention to something – a letter you are writing to a friend, a business associate you are speaking with, or a soup you are making for your family – and to be aware that as you are giving your attention, you are also giving your love. In this way, you will enjoy the experience more, by calling attention by its rightful name – love. The experience of the recipients of your attention will also be enhanced – the letter will be empowered, your associate will feel your sympathy, your soup will be filled with chi (good energy.)

Also, be aware of the attention that is given to you today and recognize it as love. See how this new definition affects your appreciation level of those around you and their appreciation of you.

Find six instances during the day in which you recognize that when you give your attention, you are giving your love.

Say the symbol statement, *"I love what I do and I do what I love. I am a happy person. The happier I am, the happier I get!"* Smile and feel it!

Conclusion

As you finish this book, it is my hope that you will take these thirty exercises, with you into the future. They are based on truth at its highest level. They will serve you well, as they have served me.

From family matters to playing tennis, from creating art to building a business, I have improved my life immensely by being happy. Occasionally, I fall overboard in the midst of my strivings and get caught up in circumstances, leaving happiness behind. Once I realize this, I figure out where I took a wrong turn, change course, climb back in the happiness boat, and sail away.

Happiness is a discipline. It is to obey the heart, with the guidance of the head, and the heart only asks that we be happy!

Now you know the importance of living happy and how to do it. All you have to do is do it! Remember; live HAPPY; life is better that way!

If you liked *The Importance of Living Happy,* please be kind enough to post a short review of it on Amazon. Thank you.

I am also happy to report that I have gathered 365 happy thoughts from my King Features syndicated panel and created a wonderful companion book to this one. It is called: *365 Reminders of The Importance of Living Happy,* wonderful thoughts to tickle any heart. It may be found on my website or on Amazon. Enjoy!

About the Author

Sally Huss

    "Bright and happy," "light and whimsical" have been the catch phrases attached to the writings and art of Sally Huss for over 30 years. Sweet images dance across all of Sally's creations, whether in the form of children's books, paintings, wallpaper, ceramics, baby bibs, purses, clothing, or her King Features syndicated newspaper panel "Happy Musings."

    As an author/illustrator of children's books, Sally creates books to uplift the lives of children. She does this by giving them tools to overcome obstacles; by helping them value themselves and others; and by inspiring them to be the best that they can be. Her catalog of children's books now exceeds 100.

    Sally is a graduate of USC with a degree in Fine Art and through the years has had 26 of her own licensed art galleries throughout the world.

    For more information on Sally: www.sallyhus.com.